P9-DOD-181

How Shall We Pray?

30 Steps to Prayer

James F. Gaffney

Resurrection Press
An Imprint of
CATHOLIC BOOK PUBLISHING CO.
Totowa • New Jersey

First published in September 2004 by Resurrection Press, Catholic Book Publishing Company.

Copyright © 2004 by James F. Gaffney

ISBN 1-878718-94-0

Library of Congress Catalog Number: 2004106633

Cover design by Beth DeNapoli

Printed in Canada.

1 2 3 4 5 6 7 8 9

Contents

INTRODUCTION

INTEREST in spirituality has increased dramatically in the last few years. In a variety of forms and expressions, spiritual concepts have been applied to corporations, recovery programs, self-help groups, personal finances, and even advertising. People go to great lengths to feel "spiritual" and can end up doing some pretty weird stuff "to get the feeling." Spirituality has become a buzzword, a fad that people do, pretty much the same way they "do lunch."

There is the mistaken notion that a genuinely spiritual life can exist apart from religion, community, and faith. In the modern mindset, spirituality is a stand-alone activity in which one occasionally engages as a medicinal remedy for the soul. Although some might consider this to be a head-clearing, revitalizing tonic, a truly spiritual way of life is much more. It transforms and changes the whole person, touching the core of our humanity—our souls. It requires change, sacrifice, discipline, and thought. Like an artist's chisel to granite, the soul slowly yields to the small chippings that come from God's call to holiness. Bit by bit, we are formed in His image and likeness. Spirituality has a goal and purpose, one that carries us from this life to the next.

This book provides some thoughts and suggestions for developing and enhancing our prayer life. It does require some thought so that we make the most of the spiritual exercises we choose to do to best address the needs of our souls. They are not meant to be used all at once. Some might be used regularly, some periodically, others when we need a boost. Some might be used just when we struggle with a difficult time, a challenging stage of growth or the need to be closer to God.

We are a praying community. In sharing that bond, we pray for and with each other as we journey the road of faith together. As Christians, we have both a particular dignity and destiny that are ours by virtue of our Baptism. We are called to follow the Lord, to be living witnesses of His love. As such, our lives have a meaning and purpose greater than ourselves, greater than our work, greater than life itself. That purpose, that mission is to be one with God. Simply stated, we are to journey through this life to Heaven.

Prayer is the foretaste of Heaven. When we pray, we unite ourselves to God. We follow the mandate of Jesus to die to self and simply come into the Presence of God. Prayer is life giving. It is life sustaining. It is essential. When we pray, we renew our commitment to God; we renew ourselves and our determination to continue the journey, to "pick up the cross" and follow the Lord. Without prayer, we wander. We lose our sense of purpose, of direction, of mission. In fact, in a very real way, we lose ourselves, our true selves. We die.

How do you begin to pray? Only one thing is necessary: We simply become aware of the Presence of God and be still. Even for just a few moments a day. We leave behind all concerns, all worries and anxieties, all fears and simply focus on God. Nothing more. Believe it or not, God will guide and direct us. Bit by bit, we will want to spend more time in prayer—not only want to, but need to. Once aware of God's Presence, then we can present all our needs, our fears and our innermost thoughts. Give them to God and then, once again, be still. Give the Lord time to respond, time to speak to our heart. The grace and strength we need will be ours.

At times, we will feel empty. Unconnected. Lost. These are not negative things. In all things, God can work to draw us closer to Him, to increase our desire for Him, to strengthen our faith like "gold that's tested in fire." At these moments, we must persevere and trust God. Perhaps there is something in our life that we need to examine. Or we are too preoccupied to really pray. Or too tired. Or worried. Or uncertain. In those moments, rely on memorized prayers, or Scripture readings, or uplifting memories of past experiences of the Lord. God can and does work through memory and imagination and emotions. He will use any means possible to reach us, to love us, to share Himself with us.

We are that important to Him. Prayer helps us make Him that important to us.

It is very important to consult people of experience; for otherwise you will imagine that you are doing yourselves great harm by pursuing your necessary occupations. But, provided we do not abandon our prayer, the Lord will turn everything we do to our profit, even though we may find no one to teach us.
                                                —*St. Teresa of Avila*

If you have a favorite method of prayer and would like to share it with us and our readers, please write the author, c/o Resurrection Press, 77 West End Rd., Totowa, NJ 07512. Please feel free to include your address and phone number.

STEP ONE

Pray with a Crucifix

RELIGIOUS objects and art play a significant role in spirituality. But perhaps none is more important or more recognized than the crucifix. Many Catholic families have a crucifix hanging in their homes, displayed in a prominent place, a succinct reminder of the central mystery of our faith that gives life meaning and purpose. In addition to being a symbol of faith, the crucifix can also be a focal point of prayer.

Many people gaze upon a crucifix while praying. But we can try holding a crucifix while praying. The symbol itself will speak to us and inspire our prayer. The physical touch will help us to focus and concentrate our attention. The enormity of the mystery will draw us in and give our prayer depth and dimension.

The crucifix itself does not have to be elaborate. We can use the one that hangs in a room at home. The key is to make it readily accessible when praying, a regular part of devotion and prayer. The occasional use of the crucifix will add dimension and variety to our prayer life; regular use will add depth and increase our devotion to the mystery of the redemptive suffering of Jesus.

Begin with the Prayer Before a Crucifix. We often pray it at the end of the Stations of the Cross during Lent.

Look down upon me, good and gentle Jesus
while before Your face I humbly kneel and, with
**   burning soul,**
pray and beseech You to fix deep in my heart live-
**   ly sentiments**
of faith, hope, and charity; true contrition for my
**   sins,**
and a firm purpose of amendment.
While I contemplate, with great love and tender
**   pity,**
Your five most precious wounds, pondering over
**   them within me**
and calling to mind the words which David, Your
**   prophet, said to You, my Jesus:**
"They have pierced My hands and My feet, they
**   have numbered all My bones."**

During the day, we could carry a small cross in pocket or purse and be reminded frequently of the Lord's Presence in everyday life. Or we can consider displaying the crucifix in a more prominent place at home. Even at work, we might keep a crucifix or cross on our desk or in our work area or vehicle. That simple symbol will help us to frequently turn our attention during our busy days to the Lord, much like the monks who permeate their day with prayer and meditation.

Finally, hymns that refer to the cross, such as "Lift High The Cross" or the traditional "That Old Rugged Cross," as well as the Scripture accounts of the Passion, are great sources of inspiration and reflection.

Carry the cross patiently and with perfect submission and in the end it shall carry you.
                                                      —*Thomas à Kempis*

STEP TWO

Attend Daily Mass

FOR many Catholics, daily Mass forms an integral part of their spiritual practice. It is the most complete and highest expression of the unity of the Church as the Body of Christ, and an essential part of the Church's prayer. Many people find that the few moments of peace they experience as well as focusing on God's Word and Sacrament set the tone for the entire day. It is easier to remember the calling we share to bring the Gospel to the world if we hear it each day.

The pace of daily Mass is different than that of a Sunday liturgy, much like a visit with the whole family on Sunday compared to a visit with just one or two relatives. With fewer people in Church, especially in the early morning, the tone is often more subdued and quiet. Many people find that it contributes to their meditation and prayer.

We gather together as a Church community to pray with each other as well as for each other. Our presence at Mass supports others as we walk our journey of faith. The readings and Holy Communion also highlight the importance of community. The Mass puts us in the flow and rhythm of the Church's daily life as the community prays for the needs of all people. One of my pastors encouraged retired people to come to daily Mass to help with the work of the Church in praying for local, national and worldwide needs. No one's life is useless and no one lacks purpose as long as we have each other.

The Eucharist provides a centering point for our day, setting a tone that permeates all we do. Going to Mass even once or twice a week is helpful, allowing us to draw on the spiritual wealth of the Church through Scripture and Communion. Even if we are physically unable to attend, we can still benefit from reading the Scriptures of the day, and making a spiritual communion.

To derive the greatest benefit from Mass, a little preparation goes a long way. Review the readings, focusing on the theme or special celebration for the day. Make the Communion fast a conscious fasting, realizing that the preparation is for receiving the Lord in Holy Communion. Arrive a little early for some quiet time to settle your thoughts and emotions and to be more alert to what is happening. If there is music, sing the hymns as prayers. If needed, consider volunteering to serve as a lector, or leader of song, Minister of Communion, or even a choir member for funerals. Take home one point of the Mass from the prayers, readings, or homily and use it for meditation and reflection during the day.

Finally, for a change of perspective, attend Mass in another parish, especially if you are fortunate to be near an ethnic parish. Other customs and traditions often offer us insights into our own spiritual practices.

Holy Communion is the shortest and safest way to heaven.

—*Pope St. Pius X*

STEP THREE

Pray the Liturgy of the Hours

THE Liturgy of the Hours, formerly called the Divine Office, is the official prayer of the Church. Priests and religious and many of the laity pray each "Hour": Morning, Evening and Night Prayer, Office of Readings and Prayer during the Day. Through prayer, each day is sanctified as an offering to God so that all that we do is a living out of God's will, furthering God's Kingdom on earth. This prayer gives the common voice of the Church a structure within which the unity of the Church is directed toward the goal of holiness. If the Mass is the efficacious sign of unity in the Church, then the Liturgy of the Hours is the efficacious prayer that guides our search for holiness.

The Hours use the psalms. Psalms are prayers of the heart. When we pray them, it is like reading someone's prayer journal in which the person expresses in verse a relationship with the Lord. Psalms capture the wide range of human emotion as they also praise and glorify God. We pray not only for ourselves, but also for the whole Church as the Mystical Body of Christ. Some parishes pray Morning Prayer before the morning Mass.

Several versions of the Church's prayer are available. The one-volume *Christian Prayer* contains the "hinge hours" of Morning and Evening Prayer, a selection of the Office of Readings as well as Night Prayer. The four-volume *Liturgy of the Hours* contains all the Hours. There is one volume for Advent and Christmas, one for Lent and Easter and two that split the thirty-four weeks of Ordinary Time. Other versions are dedicated to particular hours, seasons or even translations of the Psalms.

Some people might construct their own morning and/or evening prayer, especially as a family. These prayers can have particular meaning and importance during special seasons, important holidays, birthdays, anniversaries, etc. The sense of the community prayer of the family carries over to the community prayer of the Church. A parish priest, deacon, or religious can offer guidance in how to say this prayer of the Church.

The Divine Office is one of the most excellent works in which we can be engaged, as the Divine Praises, are celebrated in it. It is an employment fit for angels, and therefore it ought to be recited not by constraint or custom, but by choice, and with the application of our whole soul.

—St. Mary Magdalen de Pazzi

STEP FOUR

Pray with a Scripture Passage

SCRIPTURE is the written record of a people's experience of God. The stories are timeless, offering spiritual insight and moral guidance to all people. They are made of the "stuff" that is rooted in human life and endeavors and often mirror to the reader personal aspects of life. With such universal application, Scripture opens an avenue of growth and insight that cannot be exhausted. Use a good translation of the Bible. The readings used at Mass are from the New American Bible, but there are other translations as well. Ask your priest for help in choosing one.

One way of praying with Scripture is to pick a favorite passage or story and read it often. After a few moments of reflection, we can jot down whatever ideas, images or insights come to mind. By repeating this process over and over, we will become familiar with the nuances of the story, finding its patterns in our own life. This can be particularly fruitful when we pick a passage that speaks to our life and with which we closely identify.

Another variation of using Scripture in prayer is to collect different versions of the same passage, written or artistic. For example, look for one of the psalms in different translations, put to music, or depicted in art. If one passage is of particular significance, consider having it printed and framed. Perhaps find a symbol or a modern version of a story such as the Prodigal Son or the Good Samaritan. By actively immersing ourselves in Scripture, we join our experience of God with those who have gone before us and follow the road that they have journeyed so long ago.

Finally, studying Scripture formally helps us to better understand the meaning and message of God's Word. Using a good self-study guide, or attending classes can best direct our search for a better and clearer understanding. Many parishes also sponsor Bible study groups in which people learn more about Scripture as well as share their personal insights.

. . . among all the Scriptures, even those of the New Testament, the Gospels have a special preeminence, and rightly so, for they are the principal witness for the life and teaching of the incarnate Word, our Savior.

—*Vatican II*, Dogmatic Constitution on Divine Revelation (Dei Verbum), *18*

STEP FIVE

Pray with a Theme

A NOTHER way to focus our prayer is to pick a theme. Write out the theme in whatever form best captures it. The theme can be expressed as a word, sentence, paragraph, symbol, idea or theological concept. Develop it by looking for it in Scripture, listening for it in prayers at Mass, using it in personal prayers, finding spiritual reading dealing with it, etc. A theme will provide a center around which to organize prayers and reflection, choose spiritual resources and focus attention for a period of time. Once you have a sense that the theme has been exhausted, move on to something else. The material collected might be a great addition to your prayer scrapbook (see page 30).

Consider creating a calendar for the coming year, assigning a theme to each month. Each theme could be a word or two on the calendar, or it might be one provided by a spiritual organization, a diocesan program, or a parish theme or retreat. And remember: Themes can change as need and circumstances demand. The important characteristic of a good theme is that it helps us focus our prayer life and grow spiritually, making us more aware of our relationship with God. We are not trying to create a literary masterpiece or creative display of spiritual vision. A theme gives us an opening through which we more enthusiastically and deeply encounter God.

When we have to speak to others on spiritual matters, we ought first speak of them to God in prayer, and empty ourselves of our own spirit, that we may be filled with the Holy Spirit, which alone illuminates the mind and inflames the will.

—St. Vincent de Paul

STEP SIX

Relive the Sacraments

SACRAMENTS are not once-and-done events. As significant moments in our faith journey, they can be recalled and revisited in the same manner that one recalls a wedding, birth, death, special experience, visit, trip, etc. Reliving these moments stirs up memories and feelings that again bring the moment to life and with it the joy and happiness we experienced. This too is true with sacraments. The grace of each sacrament is always at work in our lives. By recalling the sacrament and learning more about it, we gain new insights that were not possible at the time we received the sacrament. Our vision and understanding is blessed by age and experience. By focusing on the meaning of the sacrament for us in the present moment we renew that particular power of God at work in us and can recommit ourselves to living graced lives. For example, we can renew our Baptismal promises, pray for the gifts of the Holy Spirit in Confirmation, rededicate ourselves to Marriage or Holy Orders, recommit ourselves to Christ in the Eucharist or thank God for His mercy and love in Reconciliation or Anointing of the Sick.

Preparing to receive the sacraments can also be a step in deepening our spiritual life. At times, receiving the sacraments can be a dramatic occasion; other times, it is part of our regular routine. But by prayer, study, and contemplation of the mysteries of grace we receive, our own sense of God's Presence in our life grows. Even when we help someone else prepare to receive one of the sacraments, our witness to faith helps us reflect on, out loud or by example, the importance of God's love.

A good book or article on sacramental theology will help us understand the doctrinal aspect of the sacrament. We might look for Scripture readings related to the sacrament. Perhaps we could find or request copies of certificates of the sacraments we have received. If you were a sponsor in the past, renew the relationship with the person sponsored. In each of these ways, we can relive these moments of grace and once again benefit from the saving work of God in our lives.

The Church constantly draws her life from the redeeming sacrifice; she approaches it not only through faith-filled remembrance, but also through a real contact, since this sacrifice is made present ever anew, sacramentally perpetuated, in every community which offers it at the hands of the con-

secrated minister. The Eucharist thus applies to men and women today the reconciliation won once for all by Christ for mankind in every age.

     —*Pope John Paul II,* Ecclesia de Eucharistia

STEP SEVEN

Nurture the Soul

POETRY, story, art, movies, music, and theater all have the power to touch us in the deepest parts of our soul. Besides nurturing the soul, they also put us in touch with the soul's needs, activities, movements, and expressions. Spirituality is not just about saying prayers and practicing religion; it is concerned with our sensitivity to the spiritual realities that surround us, influence us, nurture us, and motivate us. The care of our spiritual self is more than partaking in entertainment. It is recreation, that is, a re-creation of our inner life. Like priming a pump, attention to the nonphysical side of our lives draws us more deeply and more readily into the religious. We see more clearly the finger of God in the events of our lives and come to follow Him with a deeper clarity and fidelity. Like the layers of an onion, we move through our outer resistance into the softer, gentler parts of our soul, finally discovering the abiding Presence of God within.

Taking time to enjoy the arts is a primer for religious expression. When our spiritual life seems sluggish or at a standstill, a visit to the museum, bookstore, theater, or concert hall can refuel our energy and our enthusiasm.

The journey inward is rarely straight and predictable. We can direct our focus by using the natural and spiritual gifts of God, reinvesting them in our quest for Him.

The link between good and beautiful stirs fruitful reflection. In a certain sense, beauty is the visible form of the good, just as the good is the metaphysical condition of beauty. This was well understood by the Greeks who, by fusing the two concepts, coined a term which embraces both: kalokagath'a, *or beauty-goodness. On this point Plato writes: "The power of the Good has taken refuge in the nature of the Beautiful."*

—*Letter of His Holiness Pope John Paul II to Artists, 1999*

STEP EIGHT

Use a Journal

A JOURNAL is more than a diary or a day-to-day record of what we did. A journal is a collection of prayers, thoughts, ideas, memories, letters, ramblings, intuitions, faith experiences, inspirations, and so much more. While there are many types, styles, and methods of journaling, the best way is the one with which we are comfortable and to which we return frequently.

An essential characteristic of a journal is its broad definition of purpose and content. When writing in a journal, we are actually tapping into a spiritual process within ourselves that is ongoing and vibrant. Our meditative self has a life and a movement all its own that we must respect. We can only observe this process, recording just what we think, experience and remember. It is not a process that we control, nor are we able to predict where it will lead. By inner attentiveness, this meditative life will reveal to us a deep part of ourselves that resists our conscious efforts, often using dreams, reflections, memories and feelings. After becoming quiet and settled, we direct our awareness to this inner life, realizing that we are journeying to a deep part of our soul.

Another component of a journal is more conscious. We can record thoughts, reflections, prayers, and ideas that inspire us or capture our attention. Some of these might be for later use, recorded as an aid to memory. Sometimes an idea, bursting with meaning, requires additional time to fully comprehend. Still others are so heavily layered that we are provided with meditative material for extended periods of time. Whatever the case, a journal is a tool that gathers together the fruits of our meditative work. It effectively presents back to us a picture of our inner life that helps us integrate the diverse aspects of the person we call "self."

There are many journaling workshops offered at retreat and renewal centers. A workshop is a good way to gain the basic knowledge to make journaling more fruitful.

My Soul is open before you. Like a blank sheet of paper.
Write on it what you will, O Lord: I am Yours.
　　　—Pope John XXIII, Journal of a Soul

STEP NINE

Record in a Prayer Log

A PRAYER log is not a journal. It more closely resembles a diary or even a "To Do" list in that it helps us accurately monitor our time in prayer as well as record thoughts that we do not want to forget. Over an extended period it can show us the amount of time we spend in prayer, the best time by actual practice, the frequency, and any progress we make.

A log helps us organize our prayer time. In it we list prayer intentions we wish to remember, thoughts and ideas to which we want to return, and ideas or inspirations that come to us in prayer. That way we can find in our prayer time stepping stones for our next encounter with God. This is especially helpful in those times in which we just can't seem to get started and our minds wander and are so easily distracted. If we were to turn to a spiritual director, the prayer log would be of great value to assess personal patterns and type of prayer. It can also motivate and encourage us by showing us, in black and white, the direction of our spiritual work and prayer.

Sections of a prayer log might include People To Pray For, Thoughts of God, Inspirations, Insights,

Random Thoughts for Later, New Connections, and I Finally Understand. Each category can be filled with whatever is most personally striking. In every return to the log or any specific category, inspiration will be created anew. These thoughts do not have to be developed or explained. The entries in a prayer log serve more to jog memory, capture insights and thoughts for later reflection, or to expand on something already considered.

Spiritual joy arises from purity of the heart and perseverance in prayer.

—St. Francis of Assisi

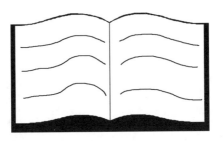

STEP TEN

Create a Prayer Scrapbook

A prayer scrapbook is like a personal prayer book. In it we can collect favorite prayers, inspirations, readings, stories, lives of saints, etc. This is a great way to begin prayer time, especially when we have difficulty getting started or when we feel particularly empty. By revisiting good moments we've had in prayer, we not only "prime the pump," but also move a step deeper in our reflections. Sometimes we need a boost. We are too tired or plain worn out. By "flooding the soul" with good thoughts, favorite prayers, and moving inspiration, we rejuvenate ourselves—and our prayer time can be more fruitful. As mentioned earlier, the scrapbook can be a place to collect prayer themes used in the past. It helps give our spiritual life continuity.

There may very well be times of dryness when we feel empty and our prayer life is seemingly at a standstill. These are important moments, too. We can record our thoughts and feelings and prayer through the dryness while respecting its presence. The object of our prayer is not to rid ourselves of these moments, but to learn from them. The lesson may very well be that of a Good Friday or Holy Saturday, essential if we are to celebrate the glory of Easter. The scrapbook serves to gather those "scraps" of insight and experience and reflect back to us, over a period of time and in a more objective fashion, whatever the Lord is telling us. Feelings of dryness are more a change of direction and new meanings than they are the absence of God. Assured of His Presence and abiding love, we can pray through these times into a new depth and dimension of our spiritual life.

He who labors as he prays lifts his heart to God with his hands.

—St. Bernard of Clairvaux

STEP ELEVEN

Go on a Retreat

A$\!$N annual retreat is a special time that can serve many purposes. It helps us evaluate our spiritual life, renew our enthusiasm, clarify our relationship with God and others, draw us more deeply into our faith, strengthen our understanding of religion, refocus our goals, discover new themes, revisit past experiences of grace, and recommit our life to God.

A retreat can be a spiritual checkup. Because of its intensity and scrutiny, retreat is a time to access our progress or lack thereof; a time to inventory the promises and intentions we kept and those we did not; a time to rest from the journey, contemplating our life and dreams and goals and desires. Heady stuff? In a way, perhaps. But actually, when we are serious about our spiritual lives, this is the process we live each day, often without conscious thought. We move on our journey a step at a time, making choices and decisions along the way. Retreat is a time to look more intently at this process, change direction, and adjust our pace so that we persevere to the end.

On a practical note, we can make a retreat last all year long. While on the retreat, we can use our prayer scrapbook. By using it, perhaps we can discern the major themes of the past year or develop one for the coming year. Maybe we could use a Scripture passage for the retreat and then develop it during the year through study, art, various translations, songs, etc. Sacraments give us ample material both for retreat and for later focusing on implementing the grace of the sacrament more consciously each day. In short, the work of the retreat can set the theme, tone, and content for the major part of our prayer life for the weeks and months afterward. By organizing and focusing our thoughts, we will tend to be more aware of the ways God works in our lives and respond accordingly.

Finally, good retreats are worth traveling for, especially if a theme or speaker is of particular interest to us. But using a retreat center each year, or staying close to home each has its own advantages. Closer to home allows for visits during the year, even if for an occasional Mass or some quiet time. Returning to the same place each year adds a sense of consistency and familiarity that helps us enter the work more quickly. In the end, the destination is a personal choice.

Nowhere can a man find a quieter or more untroubled retreat than in his own soul.

—Marcus Aurelius

STEP TWELVE

Continue Learning

MANY Catholics stop formal learning about their faith after they finish CCD, Catholic school or Confirmation class. Adult Education classes oftentimes are not well attended and usually are limited to a Lenten series. Yet when people do attend, they almost always are excited about what they learned and fully intend to learn more. Our education in faith is important. We cannot live an adult faith with a child's understanding of what it means. Understanding what we believe, and why we believe enables us to grow in our spiritual life.

Knowledge opens the door of insight, connecting us in a more intimate way to our spiritual practices and beliefs. There is so much to learn about theology, faith, spirituality, and religion. Different experiences, expressions of faith, cultural influences, and historical circumstances shape our religious practice and theological explanations. These various perspectives can deepen our appreciation for our own beliefs and help us discover their roots and nuances in our own lives. So while we share the same faith, St. Ignatius Loyola had a different perspective than St. Francis of Assisi. Those who have gone before us can teach us much about the journey of faith. Each is unique yet complements the spiritual life of the Church. By reading these and other great spiritual masters, seeking spiritual direction, and delving into theology and Scripture, we will augment our own search for God and our understanding of His mysterious ways. Take an adult education class, read a good theology book, watch a video or DVD, or subscribe to a Catholic magazine or newspaper. The more we know and understand, the more attentive and deliberate we can be in the practice of our faith.

To fall in love with God is the greatest of all romances. To seek Him is the greatest of all adventures. To find Him is the greatest human achievement.

—Anonymous

STEP THIRTEEN

Research the Life of Your Patron Saint or Parish Patron

SAINTS are ordinary people who sought to live their faith extraordinarily. In the day-to-day realities of their lives, they kept their focus on God and approached life with an attitude of faith. Their lives are more than good examples. They are a source of encouragement and hope—a kind of "If they can do it, so can we!" Each has a story to tell, and faith to share. It is not our purpose to mimic them but rather to emulate the confidence, virtue, and perseverance that underpin the spiritual life—theirs and ours.

So what's in a name? The life of a person influences us only to the degree that we know it. By learning about our patron saint or that of our parish, we become more aware of the virtue or charism that characterized the person's life, that very essence that we seek to emulate. The personal connection we have with the saint increases our consciousness of his or her life and fidelity; it is the first step in being able to put into practice the faith that the individual professed so well. Remember Confirmation and choosing a saint's name? Many of us had to write about our patron saint and why we chose a particular name. Some chose the name of a relative they admired while others chose a saint they considered heroic. We had our heroes of faith and virtue and were reminded often that we were to be like them.

Often Catholics are accused of worshiping saints. What we actually do is call upon them as members of the same Mystical Body of Christ, the communion of saints. We ask for their intercession with God on our behalf as well as for their prayers and communal support as we strive to be like them in their love of God, faith in Christ, and fidelity to the Gospel. Like master teachers, the saints show us in word and deed the way of the spiritual life. Their lives are living textbooks of faith and their stories inspire us to live our own ordinary faith in extraordinary ways.

Let us faithfully transmit to posterity the example of virtue, which we have received from our forefathers.

—St. Peter Damian

STEP FOURTEEN

Become Familiar with the History of Your Parish

MUCH of what we do in a parish builds on the work of those who have gone before. We run the school that someone else established, work at the annual carnival that began many years ago, and use church buildings built by a previous generation, paid for by their sacrifices and prayers. Even the spiritual work of evangelizing and proclaiming the Gospel is done on the foundation of faith laid by others. By knowing our parish history, we can build upon the work of the past, experiencing the continuity of faith within a living community. We come to better appreciate the contributions of others and have a better understanding of who we are as a parish community.

This is really the spiritual benefit of knowing our history: We know we are not alone in the journey. Indeed, while each person has his or her unique journey to make, we make it together. Joined in the intimate bond of faith in Christ through the Eucharist, we travel the same road while finding our own way to God. In the larger perspective, we as a Church are one community of faith. Those who have gone before us and those who will come after us all belong to Christ. Our spiritual life is strengthened by the community, supported in its struggle, and guided by its collective wisdom. Since it is through Christ, and through His Body—the Church— that we go to the Father, no one travels alone. We all need the Church.

The church building itself becomes a place of memories: milestones in our spiritual and sacramental life, significant events of the faith community, and the focal point of prayer and worship. This sacred space is a living testament to a community of faith proclaiming the Gospel. One cannot help but sense this legacy in the great cathedrals as well as the tiny chapels in remote villages. In the simplest of parish churches, this is also true, all the more so because the memory is part of the individual's lived experience. It is these memories that invigorate and renew our faith still.

He became what we are that He might make us what He is.

—St. Athanasius

STEP FIFTEEN

Be Inspired by the Themes of
a Eucharistic Congress, a World Youth Day, or
the Documents of the Church

LARGE gatherings of people at Church-sponsored events are usually well organized, planned to the last detail, and focus on a theme that often addresses issues of the day. Events such as a World Youth Day or Eucharistic Congress attract much publicity, some great speakers, incredible liturgies as well as outstanding art and music. Attending these events is like making a "super-retreat" in that they uplift, inspire, and renew our faith. If we cannot attend, however, the materials that are available can provide us with a great deal of information and a great source of inspiration and reflection for years to come. For example, in 1976 the Eucharistic Congress in Philadelphia had as its theme the hungers of the human family. One of the songs written for the Congress was "Gift of Finest Wheat," a Eucharistic hymn still in use today by many parishes, which provides a wonderful reflection on the great gift that we have received from the Lord. We might find out about a World Youth Day directly from one or a few of the youths who attend from our area or indirectly from coverage in a national magazine or diocesan newspaper. The stories of faith during this time are an inspiration like no other. These events provide a wealth of material even for those of us who cannot attend.

Another source of reflection often overlooked are the official documents of the Church such as Documents of Vatican II, papal encyclicals, pastoral letters, and various instructions. Often they contain theological explanations, spiritual exhortations, and the collected wisdom of the Church. They frequently shape the practice and beliefs of the universal Church as well as reveal the heart of the spiritual journey of the Church. By defining Herself and Her work, the Church draws its members into closer communion with each other and clarifies the work by which that same community is identified, nourished, and maintained. The more closely we identify with this work of the Church, the better our understanding of the spiritual life and mission entrusted to us.

These documents help us in two ways. First, the explanations they provide offer a great way to educate ourselves about the mission and nature of the Church as She fulfills the mandate of Jesus to preach the Gospel to the whole world. Reading the Church's own understanding of the Mass, sacraments, and mission gives us greater insight into the purpose of and need for the community of faith. Secondly, these documents give us the chance to reflect on our own role in the Church, renewing our commitment to be more involved in the life of the Church. Once we understand what the Church does and what it believes, our spiritual life changes and grows, making it impossible for us simply to warm a pew. It calls us and challenges us to be real, true, and eager disciples of Jesus.

Christianity is good news, not good advice.
—William R. Inge

STEP SIXTEEN

Pray the Jesus Prayer

IN the hectic life we lead, there is a need and always room for quiet and contemplation. In the quiet of our hearts, we find the center of our life and our being. We can clarify our purpose, redirect our thoughts to God, and find a sense of calm and peace as we turn over our lives to Him. It is a way of finding our spiritual center and reconnecting with the grace of God that dwells within.

All prayer requires a certain degree of focus and awareness, but this is especially true with the Jesus Prayer. This meditative prayer begins with our becoming quiet and still, focusing on our breathing. As we inhale, we pray: "Lord Jesus, Son of God." As we exhale, we pray: "Have mercy on me, a sinner." The prayer becomes part of our breathing and we pray as we breathe.

Remember St. Paul's admonition to pray unceasingly? This type of prayer helps us focus inward and is known as a "centering prayer." We first become aware of our surroundings, and then we focus inward as we strive to experience union with God. If it all sounds mystical, it is. As a meditative prayer, it needs to be practiced and prayed regularly. As a discipline, we develop the skill of focusing inward, recollecting our thoughts. As a prayer, it becomes intertwined with our breathing and we can fulfill Paul's desire for the Church to pray always. Much has been written about centering prayer. Before beginning this type of prayer, a little study and instruction can be helpful.

Day by day, dear Lord, of thee three things I pray:
To See thee more clearly, Love thee more dearly,
Follow thee more nearly, day by day.
       —St. Richard of Chichester

STEP SEVENTEEN

Use a Mantra or Significant Word or Phrase

SOME words or names carry special meaning for us: names of loved ones; places where we had special experiences; words of a love letter, poem, or song. We can "pack" words with meaning by the things we associate with them. In our spiritual life, a significant word or phrase can be used to capture a religious experience, an understanding, or an insight, or summarize a period of our life. The word or phrase is a reminder of that experience, drawing us back to the thoughts, feelings, tones, and moods that were part of that time. Much like a suitcase packed with clothes and necessities, a word or phrase is packed with meaning that we can open and discover again and again. That process itself leads us into new insights, thereby taking us deeper into our spiritual awareness and strengthening the personal meaning that we attach to the word or phrase. The phrase could be part of a theme we use in our prayer. The word may be the focal point of collecting prayers, readings, Scripture verses, and hymns—all ways in which we keep the word fresh in our minds and close to our hearts.

The advantage of such a practice is that it takes us quickly and more directly to a place within ourselves where we find ourselves in God's Presence—or at least we are more conscious of it. Once we feel that we have exhausted the word or phrase, or that it loses its appeal, we can place it in our prayer scrapbook as a treasured memory, a marker along our spiritual journey. Perhaps at a later time, it will be useful again, or it may take on a nuanced meaning that gives us a deeper insight into faith.

There is nothing small in the service of God.
—*St. Francis de Sales*

STEP EIGHTEEN

Return to Traditional Devotions

"IF at first you don't succeed, try, try again" could easily be adapted for those who are striving to develop their spiritual life. Like any other endeavor, often it is a matter of getting started and seeing where things lead. When we are uncertain where we should begin, it is the tried and true that offers us the best start, because sometimes what is most obvious or familiar to us is easily overlooked.

Traditional devotions are the mainstay of the Church's spiritual life. Like a favorite chair or a visit to our hometown, a return to devotions such as the Rosary, the Stations of the Cross, Benediction, Novenas and Church missions can put us back on course by giving us our bearings and renewing the foundation of our spiritual life. It's like going back to the basics. When we get lost, going back to the last known point often helps us find our way. When we are spiritually dry, or uncertain, our return to the traditional devotions that we know helps us to connect with the rhythm of the spiritual life. We reflect on the fundamental mysteries of faith: Jesus' life, death and Resurrection; God's infinite mercy and love; the community of faith; sin and grace;

salvation and redemption. These building blocks of faith are renewed within us and we can once again rebuild and strengthen our spiritual practices.

And it's important for us to note that we don't necessarily have to do these devotions the "same old way." There are many ways to pray the Rosary and the Stations. Missions are as varied as the people who preach them. And of course, as mentioned earlier, daily Mass and Communion is the mainstay of all devotions.

> *To show great love for God and our neighbor, we need not do great things. It is how much love we put into the doing that makes our offering something beautiful for God.*
>
> —*Mother Teresa*

STEP NINETEEN

Practice the Corporal and Spiritual Works of Mercy

SEMINARY students joke frequently about the old standby question asked of the many guest speakers on subjects as diverse as social justice, education, hospice, and politics: What can we as seminarians do? People often ask the same kind of question: What can I do? I am only a housewife, worker, student, retired, etc. They (and we) ask as though these were limiting factors that inhibited or even prevented them from being holy or prayerful or active in the practice of their faith. Many a saint had greater obstacles and yet overcame them to do great things. As Jesus says, "With God, all things are possible." So, what are our possibilities?

Although they are not devotions per se, the Spiritual and Corporal Works of Mercy—succinct, concrete ways that we put faith into practice—can give a boost to our spiritual life. The Corporal Works of Mercy are these: feed the hungry; give drink to the thirsty; welcome the stranger; clothe the naked; visit the sick; visit the prisoner; and bury the dead. The Spiritual Works of Mercy are these: admonish the sinner; teach the ignorant; counsel the doubtful; comfort the sorrowful; bear wrongs patiently; forgive all injuries; and pray for the living and dead. None of these requires special skills, knowledge, or ability, just a willingness to serve others. The works of mercy can meet the needs of others, even without their knowing it—more than a random act of kindness, it is a random act of faith! Expressing our own faith in such specific ways nourishes it and gives it a visible goal. We pray for *someone;* we feed *someone;* we help *someone.* All the while, it is *someone* who does the same for us.

A final thought about the Works of Mercy. When a person is really struggling with faith and trying to develop a spiritual life, the Spiritual and Corporal Works of Mercy are a wonderful kind of spiritual exercise that builds up faith and helps it grow. The Works of Mercy often show faith in action, witnessing to the power of faith to do good. In mission work, the Corporal Works of Mercy are the first steps toward preaching the Gospel. People experience the love and mercy of the community of faith so that they ask the questions that lead to faith: Why do you do this? Who is Jesus? How are we loved and saved? The Works of Mercy express the love of God and the community. We cannot help but be nourished and strengthened by practicing them.

Try to have faith instead, to do what you can and stop worrying about whether or not you're effective. Worry about what is possible for you to do, which is always greater than you imagine.

—Archbishop Oscar Romero

STEP TWENTY

Use a Different Language, Gesture, or Position

COMMUNICATION is the key to whatever type of way we live our spiritual life. We express ourselves to God and wait for God to express Himself to us. Meditation, petition, praise, or contemplation all involve communication of self to Self and person to Person. How we communicate can be as important as what we communicate. The method or means is part of the message. For example, telling someone "I love you" is different than singing the person a song that says the same thing. Although the message is the same, the method changes me, the person with whom I am communicating, and how that person receives and remembers the message. Advertising knows and uses this knowledge well.

We can apply this idea to change our prayer. Use a song instead of words, or pray in a different language, or learn a familiar prayer in Latin, the Church's official language. Find out the origin of theological words and bypass the usual way we understand their meaning. We can deepen our understanding of what we pray if we have a better knowledge of the words we use. Using a foreign language for prayers, or reading

Scripture, can offer us a new perspective, much like going to a different parish for Mass. Even without being fluent, we can get a new feel for very familiar passages and prayers.

When words fail us, or are just not adequate, gestures and positions can carry our meaning and intentions. Human expression is more than just words: We communicate with our bodies as well. Kneeling, praying with open hands, walking with the Rosary, prostration, and dance are all positions and movements of prayer that have been used for centuries in monasteries, houses of prayer, and in cultures other than our own. Gestures, so often used at children's liturgies and prayer services, help us express ourselves and focus our attention more keenly on what we say and do. Our position or posture—whether kneeling, sitting, standing, or even having a "prayer corner" in our house—helps put our minds and hearts into "prayer mode." While it may feel strange at first, we find a change in attitude and a newfound enthusiasm. In all that we do, we seek to give glory to God, expressing our love and faith in Him.

Settle yourself in solitude and you will come upon God in yourself.

—St. Teresa of Avila

STEP TWENTY-ONE

Make a Pilgrimage

A PILGRIMAGE is a trip to a shrine or holy place done for spiritual reasons. In the past it was given as a form of penance or undertaken for devotional reasons. More common in Europe than in the States, pilgrimages combine elements of a retreat, prayer, soul nurturing, and education, creating the possibility of a powerful religious experience. A journey like this can open our minds and hearts to see God in a new way, thus helping us renew and recommit ourselves to a deeper life of faith.

A pilgrimage can add a dimension to our prayer life through study, reflection, and the preparation for the trip. There are some professors who run summer pilgrimages that hold classes and assign readings so that each pilgrim will have a sense of the history, significance, and culture of the destination. Books are readily available online and at religious bookstores that provide valuable information and help us better appreciate the places we visit. While there are many shrines, churches, and holy places where people go on "official" pilgrimage, a spiritual journey can be made to anyplace of importance to us: a church with historical significance, the diocesan cathedral, a retreat center, or a place named for our patron or patroness. In this sense the destination is not nearly as important as the journey there.

Regardless of the destination, making a pilgrimage involves several steps. First, learn about the desired location: its history, ministry, and spiritual work. Then prepare whatever arrangements are necessary for travel. Pray for the success of the journey and for the graces needed. Finally, make the pilgrimage. As a unique kind of retreat, the journey reminds us of our spiritual travel through this life to the next—the preparations serve as a reminder of our prayer and vigilance for the coming of the Savior; the destination turns our thoughts to our ultimate goal of being one with God forever in heaven.

God is an infinite circle whose center is everywhere and whose circumference is nowhere.

—St. Augustine

STEP TWENTY-TWO

Fast

Fasting is a spiritual practice that is not unique to Christians. Many religions use fasting as a form of spiritual discipline and personal sacrifice. Its purpose is to make us more aware of ourselves and our relationship to God. It is a type of personal denial that we use to mirror the self-sacrifice of Jesus, offering up our efforts for a spiritual purpose. Fasting helps us realize our dependence on God and our solidarity with those who are poor and needy. We deny ourselves food—though never to a point of getting sick—for a purpose, not simply as a denial for the sake of endurance. Our fasting helps us exercise control over our body so that we can redirect our thoughts to God and reflect on His goodness to us.

Fasting can be seen in several different ways. First, it can be a form of self-denial that leads to a greater self-discipline. We strengthen our will over physical hunger in order to strengthen it over spiritual things. It is a type of training that helps develop our resolve to do the good we choose and avoid the evil we do not. It reverses the expression of St. Paul, "The spirit is willing but the flesh is weak." By fasting we strive to master the physical temptations that can distract our spirit.

Second, fasting can be an aid to prayer. Our fast helps remind us of a prayer intention or need. When we feel hungry, or tempted to eat something we have given up, we are reminded to pray for a particular intention or need. Third, fasting can be a prayer itself, a type of sacrifice we offer as a prayer of praise or thanksgiving. Fourth, we can fast as a way to make some reparation for sin. We might think of it as an act of contrition and spiritual compensation. This is especially good when we cannot make reparation directly to someone against whom we sinned. Finally, fasting can be a personal step for sacrificial giving. Operation Rice Bowl had this idea in mind when we were encouraged to eat a small meal and donate the difference in cost to a program that helped feed the hungry. We could make such a sacrifice and donate the financial cost to a charity, our parish, or to someone in need of our assistance.

Our spiritual life is enhanced when our fasting has a concrete purpose that not only encourages us to continue and persevere, but gives others the help they need. This is the tangible expression of faith and the enfleshing of the Gospel in love as we care for and seek the good of others.

You will never know that Jesus is all you need until Jesus is all you've got. —Mother Teresa

STEP TWENTY-THREE

Join a Prayer Group

IN a sense, we all belong to a prayer group that we call Church. Each week and each day we come together to pray when we celebrate the Mass. As members of the Church, we never pray alone. Even our private prayers, Rosaries and Novenas are offered in communion with the whole Church. In a community one finds strength in numbers.

Prayer groups are as varied as the people in them. Some may emphasize a particular type of prayer; others do more Bible study; still others focus on a particular saint or spiritual writer for a period of time. Whatever the form, a prayer group can be a great support in our spiritual life. By praying for and with each other, members of a prayer group not only support but also learn from one another. Personal experiences and insights, struggles and solutions can offer encouragement and information that strengthen the Church. Our personal relationship with God is often validated by the similar experiences of others. Especially in dark and arid times, times of doubt and uncertainty when we just don't feel up to it, smaller groups can help us rekindle our souls.

Prayer groups usually ask members to take turns planning the session by selecting themes, readings, or hymns or by inviting special guests. The format is informal, free flowing and confidential. Many groups will ask their parish priest to come periodically to teach, guide, and share in their prayer time. Whether for a short period of time, or as a life-long commitment, prayer groups can help us feel more a part of the larger Church community. Each person's unique relationship with God broadens the group's vision, seeing the Lord in the lives of everyone.

Prayer is to our soul what rain is to the soil. Fertilize the soil ever so richly; it will remain barren unless fed by frequent rains.

—*St. John Vianney*

STEP TWENTY-FOUR

Write Your Own Words to a Traditional Melody

IT is said, especially by choir directors, that the one who sings prays twice. The wise old pastor once added, "If God gave you a bad singing voice, sit by the tabernacle and get even!" Singing is a great part of spiritual expression and we grow up singing hymns at Mass, prayer services, and special events. The creative drive is closely bound up with self-expression. Being creative is also one of the highest ways in which we imitate God's power. It is a distinct human characteristic.

Pray twice and more by choosing a favorite melody (or if a musician, creating one), and then make up your own words and sing your prayer, like David who wrote the Psalms. These homemade songs and hymns can carry feelings, thoughts and emotions in ways that simple words cannot. Even singing your favorite hymn is a great way to pray. The music adds a depth and dimension to the words, giving them a unique and special texture. You don't have to have a great voice, or even be heard by someone else. Just sing. Chant. Put your prayers to music as it comes to you. Remember listening to a choir and being moved by the power and beauty of the words and melody? Put on a good recording of a classical piece or Gregorian chant or Handel's "Messiah." Classical and modern sacred music can set a mood for prayer, help us focus our thoughts on God, or be the means of our prayer.

Music is the language spoken by the angels.
        —*Henry Wadsworth Longfellow*

STEP TWENTY-FIVE

Give Alms

MUCH has been written and preached about tithing, stewardship, and using our gifts of time, talent, and treasure for the spread of the Gospel and helping others. That is really part of our obligation to support the Church. The sound finances of any group, especially a church, is essential to its success and well-being. More importantly, our attitude toward money reflects our values and priorities. If faith is important, then we also value the community that shares it. We give our support by our presence, our participation, and our donations.

But almsgiving is more personal and comes from our spirit of generosity, reminding us that whatever we do to the least of our brothers and sisters, we do unto Him. The word alms comes from the Greek word meaning pity or mercy. When we recognize all people as children of God, we cannot help but respond to human suffering and need. If we see ourselves as the stewards of God's gifts and blessings, then we must share what we have. It is not only ours, but God's as well. It's like spending someone else's money. We have control, but never ownership.

Almsgiving is a concrete way that we share our blessings and resources with others. It is a sign not only of our love of others in need, but also the realization that all we have ultimately comes from God and belongs to Him. In both cases we allow others to experience the goodness of God in and through the community of faith. Missionaries tell us we cannot preach the Gospel to those with empty stomachs. Physical needs must be met, echoing St. Augustine who said that grace builds on nature. Good works, generosity, and sacrifice are as much a part of the spiritual life as prayer and sacraments, and they are essential to the credible preaching of the Gospel.

We help others out of a sense of mercy, compassion, and justice. Think of almsgiving as random acts of kindness. No envelope or record keeping, no thank-you notes or recognition. Just a simple person-to-person gesture that says someone cares. Someone notices another's importance, another's worth. Faith takes these facts for granted, but in the midst of want and need, it is easy, too easy, to forget.

How do we give alms? Send a grocery card to a struggling family, help pay a child's tuition at an inner city Catholic school, make sandwiches for the homeless, or sponsor a day at the soup kitchen. Donate to a clothing drive, or pay a utility bill for a poor family. Send a child to camp, or collect toys for kids at

Christmas. There are so many needs we can fill and all we have to do is look and see. What our almsgiving represents is a sharing of our own blessings. We give more than simple help. We give hope. We fulfill our obligations of justice. We concretely show God's Providence. If done out of our own sacrifice, it is all the more meaningful. Almsgiving lets us make room for others, fulfilling the law of love: Do unto others, as you would have them do to you.

For faith is the beginning and the end is love, and
God is the two of them brought into unity.
                                        —*St. Ignatius of Antioch*

STEP TWENTY-SIX

Become a Lay Associate

MANY religious communities follow the direction of their founder or other saint, observing certain rules and spiritual practices. This formalized way of life provides a structure and rhythm that allows each member to follow in the time-tested steps of the spiritual charism of the community. Regular times of prayer, meditation, fasting, work, and spiritual reading mark out the day. This integration of community, work, and prayer makes the whole day holy, dedicating all things to God.

We do not have to be a monk or nun to observe these practices. Many of these communities have Third Orders, sometimes known as tertiaries, which enable lay people to become secular members of the religious community. In their everyday life, whether married or single, they take on some of the spiritual practices and charisms of the religious community. Sometimes they are called associate members. Most Third Orders meet regularly, attend an annual retreat, study the ideas and teachings of the community founder, and strive to live their lives in closer accord with the Gospel. Many also adopt an apostolate, or ministry, that is in keeping with the work and intention of the community.

If joining a Third Order is not possible or practical, there is always the possibility of learning about the spiritual practices of any of the great saints of the Church. Saints Dominic, Francis, Benedict, and Ignatius, to name a few, are all founders of well-known religious communities. But there are so many others. Perhaps your parish is named after a saint who wrote a good deal about the spiritual life. Your patron saint might also provide a great example to learn and follow. All the saints who wrote diaries, journals, instructions, and books can provide a wealth of material and inspiration. Through associations, parishes, religious communities, and even the internet, it is possible to find others who have the same interest as you.

Finally, consider following any one of the numerous men and women from the United States that are being promoted for sainthood, such as Father Walter Ciszek, a Jesuit priest who was imprisoned in Russia for many years and wrote two books about his experiences. His is one of many stories of faith, dedication, heroism, and sacrifice that will inspire. Getting involved in the promotion of someone toward sainthood can also be a very rewarding experience.

Jesus has always many who love His heavenly kingdom, but few who bear His cross. He has many who desire consolation, but few who care for trial. He finds many to share His table, but few to take part in His fasting. All desire to be happy with Him; few wish to suffer anything for Him.

—*Thomas à Kempis*

STEP TWENTY-SEVEN

Adopt Your Own Apostolate or Mission

FAITH is not static. It is active, requiring expression and proclamation and change. Faith needs to be announced as an invitation to discover the loving, creative power of God, offered freely to all. It demands that we who believe act, making a difference in the world because we share in that creative love of God. The struggle between sin and grace is ongoing, calling us to choose one over the other. Grace triumphs when good people act.

St. Paul wrote that the members of the Church have special gifts, each one contributing to the work of the Church. Like the parts of the body, each one individually and collectively works for the good of the whole. One for all, and all for one. What we each do reflects on the whole Church as much as what the whole Church does reflects on us. We are one, holy, catholic, and apostolic. We are sent to proclaim the Gospel message by what we say and what we do.

All of us can adopt our own personal apostolate or mission, a special project in the Church that fulfills a purpose and need. Whether in the spotlight, or behind the scenes, the work and the possibilities are always there. Programs, ministries, committees, councils, and formal groups all need our support. We can lector, sing in the choir, be minister of hospitality, be part of a bereavement team, help with religious education, or bring Communion to the sick. We can join the Knights of Columbus, Serra Club, Holy Name, or CYO. We can be part of Engaged Encounter or Marriage Prep, help with retreats, or visit those in nursing homes.

We can contribute by service to the community: Altar or Rosary Society, opening the church doors for early Mass, cleaning the church, helping in the office, doing the bulletin, working for an organization, stuffing envelopes, serving as a school or soup kitchen/food pantry volunteer, chairing a special event-picnic or Christmas gift program, and preparing holiday food baskets. There are many different ways in which we can be of service to others, most of which require only time, effort, and a willingness to serve. To serve is to give, only to receive back twice what we offer.

Dedicate some of your life to others. Your dedication will not be a sacrifice; it will be an exhilarating experience.

—Thomas Dooley

STEP TWENTY-EIGHT

Make or Repair Religious Articles

PRAYER does not require any physical object. Yes, of course, the sacraments do—oil, bread, wine, water—but prayer, as well as good works and virtue, do not. However physical things can be of help. Rosaries, statues, medals, and crucifixes all help focus our attention and can aid our reflection and meditation. Pictures and art are like family photos we keep that remind us of those we love and cherish. At times, a cross on the wall, or a statue in a room can be a visual reminder to take time from our busy and hectic lives to pray.

These things can also be a record of our history and part of our spiritual heritage. Religious art and objects express the spiritual viewpoint of those who create them, often teaching lessons of faith. By preserving them, we help preserve our past, and allow those lessons to be taught again and again.

Collecting, making, and fixing religious objects such as statues, rosaries, pictures, vessels, and vestments is a work in itself. Several organizations and religious communities collect and repair, and then donate them to missions, outreach programs, schools—anywhere that

70

has a need for them. It is easy to do, and all you need are a few simple tools. If the task requires special skills, find those who can help, especially in the area of statue and painting repairs. Schools, nursing homes, missions, and poorer parishes might benefit from your efforts. A little research will find a good home for your work.

A good deed done without love goes for nothing, but if anything is done for love, however small and inconsiderable it may be, every bit of it is counted. God considers what lies behind the deed, and not what is actually done. —Thomas à Kempis

STEP TWENTY-NINE

Use Religious Films, Music, and Art

M ANY of us remember growing up and watching classic religious movies on television, such as *The Robe, The Ten Commandments, The Greatest Story Ever Told* or *The Shoes of the Fisherman*. They were so predictably aired around Easter that they seemed almost a part of our Holy Week family ritual. With great scenery and drama these films gave us a visual picture of Biblical times and often were our primary reference point as we listened to the reading of the Passion on Palm Sunday and Good Friday.

Using religious films is part of soul nurturing, but with a definite and specific religious focus that informs and inspires. In addition to the classic and modern films that depict the life of Jesus, religious figures or events, there are also documentaries with information on the Shroud of Turin, archeology of the Holy Land, the history of the Church, and stories of great artists and religious art. These are great to use for adult education, youth groups, Christian initiation and religious education programs, and a parish night at the movies.

Spirituality has long been associated with great art, music, and theater. It seems that faith requires an outlet of expression that reaches deep within our souls. Music, religious art, and church architecture can also be great inspirations. A study of the building of the great cathedrals of Europe, any of the artists of the Renaissance, the history of stained-glass windows, or even local religious art can unearth some unusual and uplifting stories. Concerts of sacred music are entertaining and inspiring, and the stories behind the creation of the classics reveal deep faith and theological insight.

Our tradition of art in all forms is rooted firmly in our belief that creativity imitates and reflects the creative power of God. All of these wonderful artistic expressions give us a new insight and a different perspective as we contemplate the majesty and grandeur of God.

Music like religion unconditionally brings in its train all the moral virtues to the heart it enters, even though that heart is not in the least worthy.
—Jean Baptiste Montegut

STEP THIRTY

Visit Other Parishes

IN some parts of the country, this is part of people's regular practice. If you miss the 7:30 at St. Peter's, there is the 8 o'clock at St. Paul's or the 8:30 at St. Margaret's. Being part of a faith community is one thing; finding the Mass time that best fits a busy schedule is another!

Visiting other parishes can give us a different perspective. It's a different environment, a different homilist, and the experience of Mass is slightly different. Every parish (indeed, every Mass within a parish) has its own unique personality and way of worship. Especially if we feel like we are in a rut, a change of scenery can be good for the soul.

Ethnic parishes can also offer some refreshing and inspiring experiences. Music, processions, and other customs can expand our own view of things as well as help us better appreciate our heritage as a universal (catholic) Church. The Mass has been celebrated in all places, languages, and cultures, adapted to the needs, customs, art, and symbols of the local Church. It is amazing to see such similarities expressed in great diversity.

Even different regions of the country have a unique flavor to their parishes. Besides the Sunday Mass, the Sacrament of Penance, social events, Bible studies, other activities, and prayer services offer us a spiritual get-away while we are on vacation, or on a business trip. It might even be just across town or a short distance away. Looking for opportunities is essential if we want to actively pursue all that the Church offers. It is not possible for any one parish or community to meet all of our needs all the time. We need to take the time and make the effort to seek out those things that will help us develop our spiritual life. People willingly do so to find a good buy, or go to a sports event, or locate a good doctor. In the same way, we need to give our spiritual life the time and attention it deserves.

A scrap of knowledge about sublime things is worth more than any amount about trivialities.
—St. Thomas Aquinas

CONCLUSION

Be Yourself

THE heart of prayer is relationship with God—but not just an ordinary relationship. With God it is not like two friends who over the years have grown comfortable with each other. The relationship is much closer, more like breathing and air, snow and cold, or painting and paint. God knows us better than we know ourselves. Our prayer helps us become more aware of God, more able to respond to His love. We focus our attention and open our senses to drink God in, allowing Him to fashion and mold us with grace so that we become His people, His Divine Masterpiece. Like people in love who begin to look alike, adapting common mannerisms, speech patterns and thoughts, we too become like the One we love and Who loves us. We think and act and speak with the mind and heart of Christ. We seek the will of God for our lives. We do unto others as God would do. But we do more than reflect God. As St. Paul writes in his letter to the Galatians, "It is no longer I who live, but Christ living in me."

Without expression, faith can die. Our common faith in God is expressed in many ways, nurturing and advancing the community's and the individual's relationship with God. We each bring to this relationship our own experiences, emotions, knowledge, culture, preferences, needs, and contributions. All of these can be channels by which the soul is nourished as well as the way in which we express our faith and belief. We use all of our being to live, express, and strengthen the bond of love that unites us to God, and God to us.

Find your own special way of being with God. Wash linens. Decorate. Join the Serra Club, Knights of Columbus, or Cursillo. Visit a nursing home. Be a prayer partner. Help in a fund-raiser. Volunteer at a parish, school, or retreat center. Write a spiritual autobiography. Create a shrine. Renew marriage vows. Become a member of a Third Order. Collect religious music or films. Make a pilgrimage. Live and practice the faith you have been given. Let it grow with each day, sharing it with others, allowing it to be the core of your life and the joy of your soul. One day, it will be your gift to the Father who will welcome you with the words of life and love: "Well, done, good and faithful servant. Enter into the joy of Your Father!"

Suggestions for Reading

INSTEAD of the usual bibliography, here are several suggestions that are on my "must-read" list. All authors have their favorites. These are mine, with a few short notes to explain why.

1. Begin with the Catechism!

The *Catechism* has an outstanding section on prayer that covers the history of Christian prayer, types of prayer, an analysis of the interior struggles, and communal prayer. Then follows an incredible commentary on the Lord's Prayer. This section is filled with facts and insights that help us better understand the Church's rich tradition of prayer. We cannot do what we do not understand. This is a great place to start.

2. The Church Fathers

Some of the early Church Fathers write about prayer and spirituality. Their texts, especially those concerning the Eucharist, have converted more people to the Church than any other writings we possess, save Scripture. They are the great thinkers and spiritual leaders of the early Church. Their writings are time tested and carry the weight of history and tradition.

3. *The Great Saints*

So many saints have written about prayer and about the spiritual life. Some are easier to understand than others, but their writings are always worth reading. People like Francis de Sales, Thomas Aquinas, Augustine, Ambrose, Ignatius, Catherine of Siena, Teresa of Avila, to name just a few, are great sources of inspiration and knowledge. Many of their writings are found in the Liturgy of the Hours. Depending on their length, these writings may also stand alone in a single-volume form, comprise collections from individual saints, or form an anthology of a number of saints.

4. *Documents of Vatican II*

So many times people will refer to Vatican II—sometimes as a mantra (since Vatican II); other times as a label (Vatican II Church); or even as a theological reference (Vatican II changed all that)—but rarely have they actually read the documents of Vatican II. The Council had some interesting things to say about the Church, Scripture, Sacraments, the role of the faithful, etc., that have a good deal of meaning today, more than forty years after they were first written.

5. *Encyclical Letters of the Popes*

Some of the writings of the Popes have greatly influenced history as did, for example, Pope Leo XIII's

Rerum Novarum, which defended the rights of workers and helped set the stage for labor unions. Pope John Paul II has written some wonderful encyclicals, including one on the Eucharist that should not be missed. Check the Vatican website (www.vatican.va) for lists and copies.

6. Biographies of Saints

Saints are prime examples of how faith is lived. Often they were ordinary people living ordinary lives in extraordinary ways. Look for biographies of these significant men and women, both ancient and modern.

A Final Thought on Spiritual Reading

There is a good deal of spiritual writing available, and not all of it is worth the time to read. If you are going to pursue spiritual reading, do a little homework first. Not all spiritual writing is equal. Some is more academic. Antiquity is not always a guarantee of worthiness. Some modern writers are very good. A little bit of research and a few good references will help you get the most out of your reading.